Exploring
Space

Robert Snedden

Chicago, Illinois

CHILDREN'S LIBRARY

J 919.904
SNE

www.heinemannraintree.com
Visit our website to find out
more information about
Heinemann-Raintree books.

To order:
☎ Phone 888-454-2279
💻 Visit www.heinemannraintree.com
to browse our catalog and order online.

Edited by Sabrina Crewe
Designed by Sabine Beaupré
Original illustrations © Discovery Books 2009
Illustrated by Stefan Chabluk
Picture research by Sabrina Crewe
Originated by Modern Age
Printed and bound in China by South China Printing
  Company Ltd

14 13 12 11 10
10 9 8 7 6 5 4 3 2 1

Library of Congress Cataloging-in-Publication Data
Snedden, Robert.
  Exploring space / Robert Snedden.
    p. cm. -- (Sci-hi. Earth and space science)
  Includes bibliographical references and index.
  ISBN 978-1-4109-3355-3 (hc)
  -- ISBN 978-1-4109-3365-2 (pb)
  1. Outer space--Exploration--Juvenile literature.
  2. Space flight--Juvenile literature.
  3. Astronomy--Juvenile literature. I. Title.
  QB500.262.S54 2010
  919.904--dc22
                          2009013481

Acknowledgments
The author and publishers are grateful to the following
for permission to reproduce copyright material:
© ESA, NASA, French Atomic Energy Commission and
Institute for Astronomy and Space Physics/Conicet of
Argentina p. **17** (Felix Mirabel); © Royal Society
p. **15**; © ESA, NASA, STScI pp. **3** bottom, **16**; © ESA,
NASA, STScI, and the HUDF Team p. **12** (S Beckwith);
© European Southern Observatory p. **11**; © Getty
Images/Mansell pp. **8**, **42** top; © Hzenilc p. **4**; ©
Library of Congress p. **18**; © NASA pp. **3** both, **9** top,
10, **19**, **20**, **21**, **22**, **23**, **25**, **26**, **27**, **28**, **29**, **30**, **31**, **32**
both, **33**, **34**, **35**, **36**, **37**, **38**, **39**, **40**, **41**, **42** bottom,
43 both; © NASA Marshall Space Flight Center p.
24; © Shutterstock pp. **4–5** (Stephen Strathdee), **7**
(Anastazzo), **9** bottom (Zack Frank), © Bartolomeu
Velho p. **6**.

Cover photographs of an astronaut and (inset) the
Cassini-Huygens space mission reproduced with
permission of NASA.

We would like to thank content consultant Suzy
Gazlay and text consultant Nancy Harris for their
invaluable help in the preparation of this book.

Every effort has been made to contact copyright
holders of any material reproduced in this book. Any
omissions will be rectified in subsequent printings if
notice is given to the publisher.

All the Internet addresses (URLs) given in this book
were valid at the time of going to press. However, due
to the dynamic nature of the Internet, some addresses
may have changed, or sites may have changed or
ceased to exist since publication. While the author and
Publishers regret any inconvenience this may cause
readers, no responsibility for any such changes can be
accepted by either the author or the Publishers.

Contents

What is a supernova? Find out on page 16!

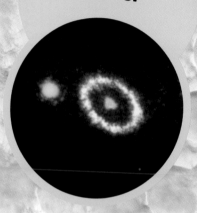

On which planet is this rover roving? Find out on page 37!

Some words are shown in bold, **like this**. These words are explained in the glossary. You will find important information and definitions underlined, <u>**like this**</u>.

Looking at the Stars

Do you ever look up into the night sky and think about what you can see there? The very first people must also have looked in wonder at the twinkling lights far above their heads.

Measuring time

- A day is the time it takes for Earth to spin once on its **axis**, or the time from one sunrise to the next.

- A month is slightly more than the time that passes from one full Moon to the next.

- A year is the time it takes for Earth to travel once around the Sun. Ancient civilizations knew when a year had passed by observing changing patterns in the stars.

Watching the skies

The movements of the Sun, Moon, and stars were important to early **civilizations**. Even before writing had developed, our ancestors could tell the time and season. They did this by recording the changing positions of the objects in the sky. As the Sun moved across the sky, the shifting shadows could be used to mark the hours of the day.

The science of astronomy

Astronomy is the study of everything that lies beyond Earth's atmosphere. It is an ancient science involving careful observations and records. For more than 2,000 years, **astronomers** have been exploring space by looking at the night skies. Over time, they have found new tools and methods for their explorations. Today we know things about space that would amaze the people of long ago who first looked at the stars.

Set in spheres

A long time ago, the scientists of ancient Greece thought that the Moon, the Sun, and the planets and stars were set in crystal spheres that revolved around Earth. These spheres were thought to make music as they turned. This idea seems odd now, but astronomy was stuck with it for centuries!

Early beliefs

For centuries, people believed that Earth was at the center of the universe. Thousands of years ago, people found patterns in the stars, called **constellations**, and named them after their gods and heroes. The night sky was like a storybook full of myths and legends.

Today, we know that the stars in a constellation have no real connection with each other. They just happen to lie in a pattern as we look at them from Earth. Present-day astronomers still use constellations as a convenient way of dividing up the night sky. All the stars and other objects in space can be placed within one of the 88 constellations.

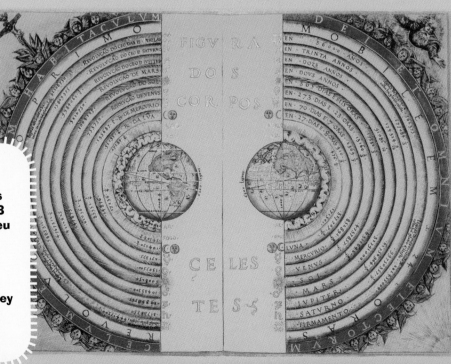

This map of the skies was made in 1568 by Bartolomeu Velho of Portugal. It shows the paths of the planets as they appeared to circle Earth.

A new idea

In about 260 BCE, the Greek astronomer Aristarchus came up with an idea that was way ahead of its time. He suggested that Earth went around the Sun. Nobody at the time believed him.

In 1543, however, Polish astronomer Nicolaus Copernicus showed that this idea was the best explanation for the way the planets seemed to move through space. Science had advanced from the time of Aristarchus, but the idea was still not widely accepted.

Word of Copernicus and his ideas began to spread, however. Then, at the beginning of the 17th century, the first known telescope was invented. Its use confirmed the ideas of Aristarchus and Copernicus: Earth was indeed in **orbit** around the Sun.

Nicolaus Copernicus (1473–1543) published a scientific **theory** that contradicted the idea of Earth being the center of the universe. His writings led to great advances in astronomy.

TELESCOPES

Telescopes are the tools of the astronomer's trade. They allow people to see farther into space than they could possibly do otherwise. The first telescopes could only magnify about 20 to 30 times. Yet that was enough to change people's view of the universe.

Galileo

In 1609 the great scientist Galileo Galilei (1564–1642) got hold of one of the first telescopes. When he looked through it, he was amazed to find that the Moon had mountains and the Sun had spots. He also saw that the planet Jupiter had moons. This was key **evidence** that not all bodies in space orbit Earth.

These are the telescopes with which Galileo discovered the moons of Jupiter.

Optical telescopes

The earliest telescopes were optical telescopes. They used **lenses** to gather and focus light. A lens is a curved piece of glass or other material that bends the rays of light to form an image. The world's biggest telescope is an optical telescope in the Canary Islands. It uses a huge mirror more than 10 meters (30 feet) across to collect light. It is used to detect planets orbiting other stars.

Radio telescopes

Many objects in space give out energy in the form of **radio waves**. A radio telescope picks up these signals and uses them to form images. The signals received by more than one radio telescope can be combined so that they act like a single, very big telescope. The telescopes below, of the Very Large Array observatory in New Mexico, USA, act together as one large telescope.

Kepler space telescope

Telescopes in space

One important tool in space exploration today is the Hubble space telescope. It was sent into space in 1990. Because it orbits outside Earth's **atmosphere**, Hubble can get clear images billions of miles into space. Several instruments on board Hubble create images that are sent to Earth. You will see several of Hubble's images in this book.

In 2009, the Kepler telescope (above) was launched into space. It is on a **mission** to look for planets like Earth in our **galaxy**. Kepler follows Earth on its orbit around the Sun. This means that Earth will never block Kepler's view of the area it is observing.

Very Large Array observatory

Turn the page to find out who the Hubble telescope is named after!

MEASURING THE UNIVERSE

As telescopes revealed more and more in the night sky, people began to wonder how big the universe actually was. Could it possibly be infinite—stretching on forever in all directions?

Mapping stars

Astronomers, such as William Herschel (1738–1822), began to make detailed star maps. Together with his sister, Caroline, also a skilled astronomer, Herschel built his own telescopes. The two began a 20-year project of star counting. The Herschels' careful records were very useful to the astronomers who came after them.

Herschel believed the universe to be a great disk of stars, called the **Milky Way**, with the Sun close to its center. Seen from Earth, the Milky Way looks like a band of pale, milky light stretching across the night sky. It is also called the "**galaxy**," from the Greek word for *milk*.

The Cosmic Background Explorer **satellite** (COBE) captured this view of our Milky Way galaxy.

The nebulae discovered by today's powerful telescopes are vast clouds of gases and dust, billions of miles from Earth. The Horsehead Nebula, shown here, is one such dust cloud.

Beyond the Milky Way

Later astronomers began to realize that there were other galaxies beyond the Milky Way. Telescopes had shown cloudy patches of light in the night sky, called **nebulae**. In 1923 astronomer Edwin Hubble (1889–1953) used the most powerful telescope of the day to calculate the distances to various nebulae. He found they were galaxies in their own right. The universe was vast beyond imagining.

Farther and faster

Edwin Hubble's studies of the stars led him to another amazing find. The galaxies he discovered weren't staying still. They were rushing away from us and from one another. Hubble then realized something important. **The more distant a galaxy is, the faster it is moving away from us**. This discovery gave astronomers a new tool for measuring the distances to the farthest objects we can see.

Distant stars

The distances between stars are immense. Trying to measure them in miles would mean using huge numbers. Instead, astronomers use the **light-year**. This is the distance that light travels in one year. <u>**Light travels at a rate of 300,000 kilometers per second (186,000 miles per second)**</u>. This means it travels about 9.5 million million kilometers (6 million million miles) in a year. Proxima Centauri, the nearest star other than our own Sun, is more than four light-years away.

Bright stars

Astronomers can calculate the distance to the stars by their brightness. They work out how bright the star is compared to the Sun. Then they determine how far away it would have to be to look as bright as it does in the night sky.

This is the Hubble space telescope's view of nearly 10,000 galaxies. The telescope looked deep into the universe, cutting across billions of light-years. The smallest, reddest galaxies may be among the most distant known.

Parallax

Another way of measuring distance is by **parallax**. Parallax is the way an object appears to shift its position when it is seen from different angles. Without you even thinking about it, your brain uses parallax all the time to work out which objects are close by and which are far away.

Astronomers use parallax to measure star distances. They take a photograph of part of the night sky. Then they wait six months until Earth is at the opposite end of its **orbit** around the Sun. They take another picture of the same area of sky and measure how the stars have changed position. From this they can work out their distance. Parallax observations from Earth can measure distances accurately to about 160 light-years.

Across space and time

Some of the brightest stars in the sky are hundreds of light-years away. When we look at them, we don't see them as they are now. We see them as they were hundreds of years ago, when the light from them began its long journey across space.

Try it: parallax

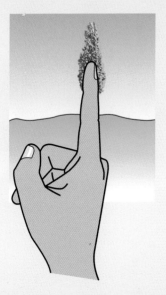

Hold up a finger and, with one eye closed, line up the finger with a more distant object, such as a tree. Now, without moving your finger, look at the object with only the other eye. It is no longer lined up. The closer your finger is to your eyes, the more the finger appears to shift. This is the parallax effect.

The beginning of the universe

We read on page 11 about Edwin Hubble's studies in the 1920s. He found that the galaxies were rushing apart. This suggested that the universe was expanding. So how small was the universe to begin with? And when did it begin?

Most astronomers today believe that the universe had its beginning around 14 billion years ago. At the time, they say, all of the material in the universe was squashed into an **infinitely** small point called a **singularity**. The singularity is an idea that is hard to understand. Everything was contained in it. Before the singularity, there was no **matter** (substances), no energy, no space, and no time.

The Big Bang theory

No one knows where this singularity came from. And no one knows why it suddenly and very rapidly began to increase in size. This sudden expanding of the universe from a tiny point is known as the Big Bang. A "big bang" perhaps isn't the best way to describe this **theory**. The universe didn't blow up with a big bang. Blowing up like a balloon would be closer. According to the Big Bang theory, the universe balloon is still expanding.

Imagine the universe is a loaf of bread with raisins in it. The raisins are close to each other in the uncooked dough (left). When the bread is baked in the oven, it expands, and the raisins move apart (right). This is what happens to galaxies and other objects in space as the universe expands.

Stephen Hawking (on the left in this photo) is one of the scientists who has helped to develop the Big Bang theory. He is shown receiving an award from the British Royal Society for his important contribution to space science.

Theories and the scientific method

Scientists follow a path to understanding and knowledge called the scientific method.

- First they identify a question or problem to be solved.
- Then they form a possible explanation. This is called a **hypothesis**.
- They make observations or test the hypothesis with experiments.
- Next they organize their **data** and study the results to see if the **evidence** supports the hypothesis. If not, they may have to do some more observing or experimenting.
- If the hypothesis seems to hold true, the scientists may set out a theory based on the hypothesis.

A theory is the best explanation that can be found for why something happens. Good scientists are always prepared for the possibility that theories will have to be changed if new evidence comes to light.

Wonders of the Universe

Astronomers have discovered marvels in the depths of space. Some of the most remarkable objects of all are formed when stars die.

SUPERNOVA

When a giant star begins to die, its core, or center, shrinks. A huge amount of matter is packed into a smaller and smaller space. The core becomes very **dense** (concentrated) and very hot. The outer layers of the star collapse in. Then they bounce back from the core in an enormous explosion. For a short time, the exploding star, or **supernova**, can outshine all the other stars in the galaxy. In just a few moments, it produces more energy than the Sun will in its whole lifetime. This image (right) of the supernova known as 1987A shows the exploded star as a red blob in the center of a ring of gases.

NEUTRON STAR

After a star explodes, its dense and shrunken core remains. An exploding star three times larger than the Sun will leave behind a core about 25 kilometers (15 miles) across. This is called a **neutron star**. It is so dense that the **atoms** of the star are crushed together. If you could bring a teaspoon of neutron star material to Earth, it would weigh about 1 billion tons!

This is an artist's image of a black hole in our galaxy. The black hole is circled by a disk of fiery blue gases. The yellow ball is a companion star that orbits the black hole every 2–3 days. The black hole steals gas from the star and will eventually consume it.

BLACK HOLES

Stars that are eight or more times larger than the Sun will collapse even further, beyond the neutron star stage. In fact, they collapse so completely that they appear to vanish from the universe altogether. They leave nothing but a **black hole** in space.

The giant star may have disappeared from sight, but its **gravity** remains. The boundary of the black hole is called the **event horizon**. At the event horizon, you would need to be traveling at the speed of light to escape the black hole's pull. Once you crossed the horizon, you would never get back out. The force of gravity inside is so intense that nothing can escape it, not even light.

Turn the page to learn how we overcome the force of gravity to explore space . . .

FROM EARTH TO SPACE

We've seen how people explored space with their eyes and telescopes for many hundreds of years. Some even dreamed of leaving Earth and going into space. As time went by, people developed new knowledge and technology. These tools made that dream a reality.

Understanding gravity

Understanding **gravity** was one of the first steps to leaving Earth. Gravity is called a universal force because everything in the universe produces a gravitational force that pulls other objects toward it. **The force of gravity influences the paths that stars, planets, and other objects follow through space**. To leave Earth and reach space, we must overcome this force.

The famous scientist Isaac Newton (1642–1727) wondered what force causes an apple to fall from a tree. In a 1687 book, he wrote that there was a force—gravity—that pulls objects to the ground. He saw that this same force held the Moon in orbit around Earth.

In 1992, the spacecraft *Galileo* captured this image of the Moon in orbit around Earth.

Into orbit

An object that is thrown or **propelled** in some way becomes a **projectile**. A projectile follows a curved path as it is pulled back to Earth by gravity. The surface of Earth is also curved. If a projectile is traveling fast enough, its curved path will follow the curve of Earth. It is still falling, but now it is falling around Earth. The projectile is in **orbit**, and it has become a **satellite**.

The Moon is a natural satellite of Earth. Its orbit follows a curved path that keeps it forever falling around Earth. Human-made objects can be satellites, too. The Hubble space telescope is one of many satellites that people have launched into orbit around Earth.

For a projectile to get into orbit, it must be fired from Earth with enough power to overcome gravity. This was the challenge that faced the scientists who dreamed of spaceflight. It wasn't until the 20th century that they developed the powerful **rockets** needed to do this.

Rocket men

In 1898, Konstantin Tsiolkovsky, a Russian teacher, wrote about using rockets for spaceflight. He never built any rockets, but other scientists used his ideas. Two of these were Hermann Oberth in Germany and Robert Goddard in the United States. Working separately, they developed the first modern rockets in the 1920s and 1930s.

This photograph shows Robert Goddard with his first successful rocket in 1926.

Modern rockets

The development of modern rockets continued throughout the 20th century. The first rocket that flew high enough to get into space was a missile launched by Germany in 1942. This was one of the most important developments in space exploration. Eventually, it enabled scientists to start sending first objects, and then people, into space!

The first rockets

The earliest rockets may have been made in China as long ago as 200 BCE. They were not very powerful or accurate, and they certainly couldn't reach space!

How rockets work

A rocket is actually one of the simplest of all engines. Have you ever blown up a balloon and then let it go and watched it fly around the room? The air rushing from a balloon provides the **thrust**, or push, that sends it on its way. A rocket engine works the same way.

Combustion, or burning, takes place when fuel is ignited (lit) and reacts with oxygen. A space rocket carries an oxidizer, which is a chemical that supplies oxygen. The oxidizer and the fuel supply together are the rocket's **propellants**.

The propellants are burned inside the combustion chamber of the rocket engine. This combustion produces very hot gases. These gases rush out through a nozzle at the rear of the rocket. The force of the gases rushing out from the nozzle produces the thrust that pushes the rocket forward.

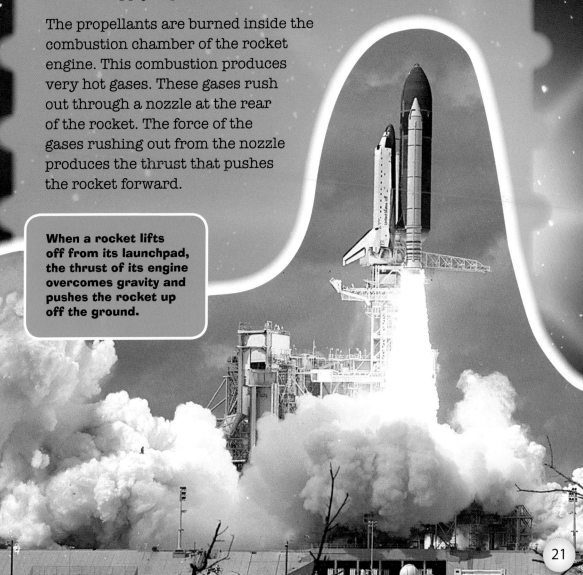

When a rocket lifts off from its launchpad, the thrust of its engine overcomes gravity and pushes the rocket up off the ground.

The first satellites

The first satellite, *Sputnik 1*, seemed to take everyone by surprise. It was hard to imagine that humans had sent an object hurtling around Earth! *Sputnik 1* traveled at over 29,000 kilometers per hour (18,000 miles per hour). One month after its launch, the USSR launched a second satellite, *Sputnik 2*. This brought another surprise. Inside was a dog called Laika—the first living thing to reach space from Earth. Laika did not survive the trip into space. Overheating and the stress of space travel caused her death shortly into the flight.

The space race begins

On October 4, 1957, the USSR (now Russia) used a rocket to launch the first human-made satellite, *Sputnik 1*, into orbit around Earth. It was the beginning of a time called the "space race," when the United States and USSR competed to launch satellites and people into space.

Sputnik 1 was 58 centimeters (23 inches) across and weighed 83.6 kilograms (184 pounds).

During the 1960s, NASA scientists controlled spaceflights from the Mission Control Center in Houston, Texas.

The United States joins the race

The United States launched its first satellite, *Explorer 1*, on January 31, 1958. The same year, on July 29, the U.S. government set up the National Aeronautics and Space Administration (NASA). This agency ran the U.S. space program. Soon the USSR and the United States were making regular satellite launches. In 1961, U.S. president John F. Kennedy set NASA the task of landing astronauts on the Moon.

New discoveries

Early satellites gave us new knowledge about Earth and the **Solar System**. The satellites, for example, had instruments to detect **radiation** in space. One of the first discoveries was that belts of radiation, called the Van Allen Belts, surround Earth. Radiation can damage instruments and make people sick. The belts would be harmful to any astronauts who spent too long traveling through them.

GOING TO THE MOON

The Huntsville Times

Man Enters Space

'So Close, Yet So Far,' Sighs Cape

U.S. Had Hoped For Own Launch

Soviet Officer Orbits Globe In 5-Ton Ship

Maximum Height Reached Reported As 188 Miles

Hobbs Admits 1944 Slaying

Praise Is Heaped On Major Gagarin

To Keep Up, U.S.A. Must Run Like Hell

Newspapers across the world announced the news that a person had gone into space for the first time ever.

Before anyone could land on the Moon, space scientists had to work out how to send people safely into space. Soon after the first **satellite** launches, both the United States and the USSR were making plans to do just that.

First person in space

The USSR was the first nation to build a space **capsule** that was safe for humans. It also produced a **rocket** powerful enough to send the capsule into **orbit**. So it turned out that the first person in space was Yuri Gagarin from the USSR. He made a single orbit of Earth in *Vostok 1* on April 12, 1961.

Blue Earth

Yuri Gagarin was the first person ever to see Earth from space. He radioed ground control, saying: "Earth is blue. How wonderful. It is amazing."

Gagarin's flight lasted for 108 minutes and reached a height of 327 kilometers (203 miles) above Earth. Gagarin parachuted back to Earth after the capsule had reentered Earth's **atmosphere**.

Project Mercury

The first of the U.S. space programs to carry people into space was Project Mercury. In May 1961, Alan Shepard became the first American into space, but his Mercury craft didn't go into orbit. John Glenn was the first American to orbit Earth, on February 20, 1962. Three more successful Mercury flights followed.

Walking in space

In March 1965, Alexei Leonov of the USSR became the first person to go outside of a spacecraft in space. This is called an **extravehicular activity**, or EVA. When astronauts leave their spacecraft, they rely on their spacesuits for protection. Today's spacesuits, such as the one (below) worn by Winston Scott on an EVA, are like mini-spacecraft. They are fitted with oxygen, refreshments, heating and cooling equipment, and even toilet facilities.

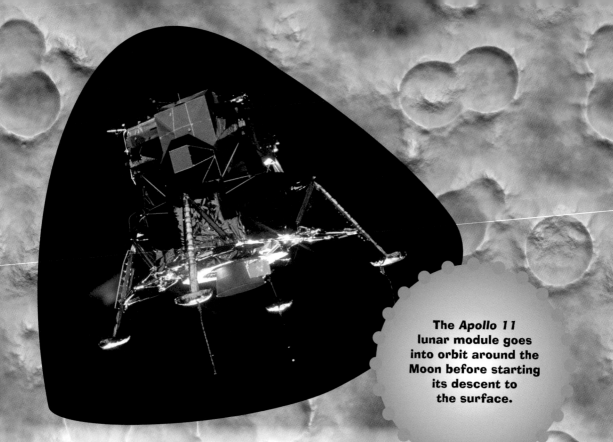

The *Apollo 11* lunar module goes into orbit around the Moon before starting its descent to the surface.

Project Gemini

The next American space program after Mercury was Project Gemini. Ten Gemini **missions** in 1965 and 1966 prepared NASA, its astronauts, and its spacecraft for a Moon landing.

During these missions, astronauts learned to change course in their capsules so they could meet and join up with other spacecraft. The Gemini missions also showed that people could survive in space long enough for a journey to the Moon.

Project Apollo

The Apollo program was the next group of missions. During these flights, astronauts tested the new Apollo spacecraft. *Apollo 10* made an orbit of the Moon. It tested the process of separating the landing craft, or lunar **module**, from the main capsule, or command module. After this final test flight, NASA was ready to try for a Moon landing.

Landing on the Moon

On July 16, 1969, *Apollo 11* astronauts Neil Armstrong, Edwin "Buzz" Aldrin, and Michael Collins were blasted into space. After just twelve minutes, the spacecraft was in orbit around Earth. Three days later, it was in orbit around the Moon.

On July 20, Armstrong and Aldrin separated the lunar module from the command module and landed it on the Moon's surface. Neil Armstrong emerged from the lunar module, becoming the first person to set foot on the Moon. He and Aldrin spent nearly a day on the Moon. They set up experiments and collected rock samples. Then, just as planned, they blasted off in the top section of the lunar module to rejoin the command module in space.

The astronauts returned safely to Earth on July 24. The race to the Moon had come to an end.

Neil Armstrong took this photograph of Buzz Aldrin standing on the Moon. You can see Armstrong and the lunar module reflected in Aldrin's visor.

Astronaut David Scott sets up scientific equipment on the Moon during the *Apollo 15* mission.

End of the Moon missions

During the 1960s and 1970s, there were several more visits to the Moon in Apollo spacecraft. On these missions, astronauts performed experiments and collected samples of rock. Since Apollo, however, no one has been back to land on the Moon.

Moon discoveries

Scientific studies from the Apollo missions showed that the youngest Moon rocks are nearly as old as the oldest Earth rocks. There is no wind or rain on the Moon, so there is nothing to wear away the rocks. But **asteroids** and meteors once pounded the Moon, leaving the craters (pits) we see today. No trace of any life has ever been found in the Moon rocks, but there is the possibility of water in the form of ice.

Lighter on the Moon

The surface **gravity** on the Moon is only one-sixth that of Earth. Gravity determines your weight. So if you weigh 60 kilograms (132 pounds) on Earth, you would weigh 10 kilograms (22 pounds) on the Moon!

Future Moon visits

With Project Constellation, NASA is building a new generation of space vehicles. They are scheduled to begin missions in about 2015. As well as carrying out missions in Earth orbit, Constellation will also take people back to the Moon for the first time in almost 50 years.

Project Constellation will use two space vehicles: the Orion Crew Vehicle and the Altair Lunar Lander. Orion will be joined with Altair. Together they will fly to the Moon, where Altair will separate and descend to the surface. If all goes well, the return to the Moon should happen in about 2020. Altair missions will explore the Moon's **polar regions**. There may be frozen water there. Some polar regions also receive almost constant sunlight, which could provide energy. These resources would make the polar regions the best places to build Moon bases in the future.

The Orion Crew Vehicle is the capsule in which future astronauts will travel from Earth into Moon orbit and back.

Shuttles, Satellites, and the Space Station

After the Moon landings of the 1960s and 1970s, space exploration took a different direction. NASA and other space agencies focused on space laboratories, **satellites**, and new ways of getting to and from space.

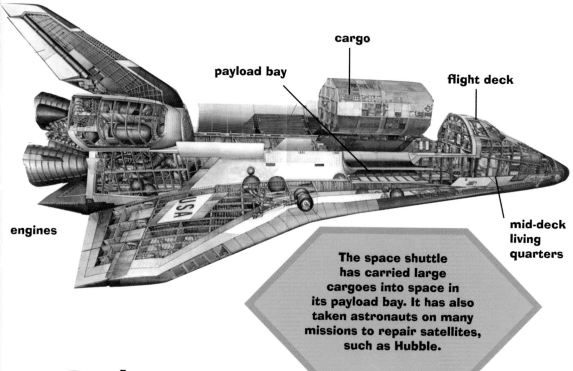

payload bay

cargo

flight deck

engines

mid-deck living quarters

The space shuttle has carried large cargoes into space in its payload bay. It has also taken astronauts on many missions to repair satellites, such as Hubble.

Back and forth

"Shuttle" means to go back and forth, and that's what the space shuttle did. Launched in 1981, it was the first reusable spacecraft. The shuttle was launched by a **rocket**, but it landed back on Earth like an airplane. The space shuttle fleet has performed more than 100 **missions** of great value to space exploration.

Turn the page to read all about the ISS!

The shuttle has enabled scientists to go into space and carry out experiments. It has also carried supplies and astronauts to the International Space Station (ISS).

New space vehicles

NASA plans to replace the space shuttle fleet with new space vehicles. We read on page 29 about Project Constellation's Moon missions. The new space vehicles will also take over the shuttle's duties. The Constellation spacecraft should be ready for service in about 2015.

Satellites

Satellites have come a long way since the days of *Sputnik 1* and *2*. Today there are hundreds of satellites in **orbit** around Earth. Hubble and the ISS are both satellites. There are many types of satellite, including:

- Communications satellites that send radio, TV, and other signals back and forth;

- Astronomical satellites that observe other planets and **galaxies** to gather knowledge about the universe;

- Weather satellites that gather information about Earth's climate and weather patterns.

Some satellites go into deep space to orbit other planets. You can find out more about these and other **space probes** on pages 34 to 37.

NASA is designing new launch vehicles for Project Constellation. The Ares V will carry cargo into space. This artist's image shows the two rocket boosters falling away after Ares V is launched into Earth orbit.

The International Space Station

The International Space Station (ISS) is an orbiting science and research center. The first part of the ISS was launched in 1998. Crew members stay on the ISS for several months. They carry out work to advance the knowledge we need for exploring space.

Life on the space station

In space, people do not feel the effects of **gravity**. Everything in the ISS floats around, and people feel as if they are weightless. This weightlessness affects many aspects of life. When an alarm wakes the crew in the morning, it rouses them from sleeping bags hooked to the wall. When they take a shower, water squirts out of a nozzle and is sucked out through a fan. At mealtimes, the crew consume soups and other liquids through straws from plastic bags. They have to eat solid food very carefully to prevent pieces from floating away and getting into the equipment.

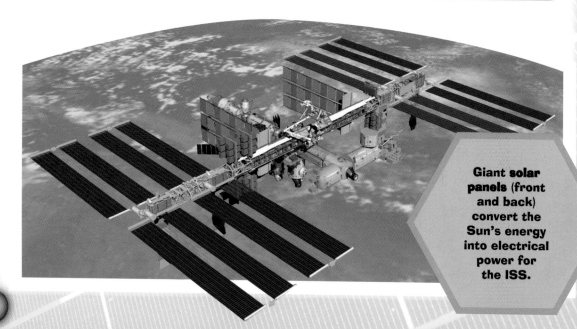

Giant **solar panels** (front and back) convert the Sun's energy into electrical power for the ISS.

Astronaut Sandra Magnus works in the research laboratory aboard the ISS. The laboratory is used for studies and experiments.

Work aboard the space station

Every crew member has a task for the day. These tasks include scientific experiments. Some of the most important experiments the astronauts carry out involve themselves. They are learning a great deal about the effects spending a long time in space can have on the human body. This will be important knowledge if future astronauts are to make the long journey to Mars and beyond.

Looking for the ISS

The ISS is visible from the ground. You don't even need a telescope to see it. The ISS is very bright and very fast, crossing the night sky in a matter of minutes. The NASA website www.jsc. nasa.gov/sightings/ will show you when you can see the ISS from your location.

Exploring Farther

So far, the Moon is the farthest place in space that any people have reached. But **space probes** have gone much farther. <u>**A space probe is an unmanned spacecraft that explores space**</u>. Several probes have traveled far across the **Solar System** and sent back important **data** about planets and other objects.

Exploring the planets

The first space probe from Earth to reach another planet was *Mariner 2*, which flew within 35,000 kilometers (22,000 miles) of Venus in 1962. Since then, a number of probes have carried out **missions** throughout the Solar System.

The Cassini-Huygens mission was launched in 1997. It flew to Saturn, entering **orbit** around the ringed planet in 2004. The *Huygens* probe landed on Saturn's moon Titan while the *Cassini* orbiter gathered data. The Cassini-Huygens mission found no **evidence** of life on Saturn. But it discovered four tiny Saturn moons that had not been seen before.

This artist's impression shows *Cassini* in orbit around Saturn.

Far from home

The probe *Voyager 1* is on an epic journey that has taken it past Jupiter and Saturn. Launched in 1977, *Voyager 1* was more than 16 billion kilometers (10 billion miles) from the Sun by 2009. It is the most distant human-made object from Earth. In a few years, *Voyager 1* will leave the Solar System altogether.

Collecting stardust

The *Stardust* probe, launched in 1999, successfully met the **comet** *Wild* 2 in 2004. It collected samples of dust from the comet's tail and sent them back to Earth in a **capsule**. The dust contained specks of material from the time when our Solar System was forming. By studying these materials, scientists can explore the early Solar System right here on Earth.

Exploring Mars

Going to Mars is no easy matter. It involves traveling hundreds of millions of miles across space. But already, a number of probes have gathered information about Mars. Some have taken detailed photographs from orbit, while others have landed to explore the surface.

The **satellite** *Mars Odyssey* was launched in 2001 to explore Mars, and it is still in orbit around the planet. This image is an artist's impression of the *Odyssey* satellite making maps of Mars.

Exploration goals

NASA has four scientific goals in its exploration of Mars:

1. to determine if life ever existed on Mars
2. to learn about the climate of Mars
3. to learn about the geology of Mars
4. to prepare for human exploration of Mars.

Landing on Mars

The first missions simply flew by Mars without landing. *Mariner 4* flew by Mars in 1965 and sent back the first close-up images of another planet. The first spacecraft landed on Mars in 1976.

Since the 1990s, several craft called rovers have not only landed on Mars but also traveled around on its surface! Some of these robot explorers are still collecting data and sending it back to Earth.

The rovers: *Spirit* and *Opportunity*

Since January 2004, the robotic rovers *Opportunity* and *Spirit* have been trekking around Mars. They use their instruments to make observations about the climate. They have tools to collect samples of rocks and soil and examine them. The rovers have sent more than 100,000 images of Mars back to Earth.

The two Mars rovers *Opportunity* and *Spirit* are identical vehicles exploring different parts of the planet.

Future Exploration

In an antimatter spacecraft like this one, people could one day travel to Mars. They would travel ten times faster than in the spacecraft we use today.

Space exploration has always advanced with new scientific knowledge. In the future, we may be able to go farther into space and learn more about it. New technology being developed on Earth will help us do that.

We still rely on **rockets** to get our spacecraft and **space probes** into **orbit** and beyond. But once we have escaped Earth's **gravity**, there are other systems we can use that can **propel** spacecraft when they are in space. New systems could give us more power and more speed than we have ever imagined.

Sailing on the solar wind

A solar sail is like a very large, very thin mirror. NASA is testing materials for solar sails that are 100 times thinner than the pages of this book. As particles (tiny pieces) of light called photons bounce off the sail, they gently push it through space. The very slight pressure of the light will slowly **accelerate** the solar spacecraft. Eventually the spacecraft could reach speeds of 90 kilometers a second (about 56 miles per second). By using **laser beams** (powerful beams of light) to boost the sunlight, scientists believe that speeds of more than 30,000 kilometers a second (18,600 miles per second) should be possible!

Antimatter engines

Antimatter may sound like science fiction, but it is science fact. Normal **matter** is what we and all the things around us are made of. You can think of antimatter as being like normal matter in reverse. Some scientists describe it as the negative of matter. Matter is a very concentrated form of energy. So if antimatter comes into contact with matter, both are instantly destroyed in a high-energy flash.

Antimatter engines could harness this energy to provide **thrust** for a spaceship. Antimatter is a possible source of power for a Mars **mission**. The antimatter for the engines would be produced using **particle accelerators.** These huge machines create particles of antimatter. It will be a long time before they can make enough to power a spacecraft.

A giant solar sail takes shape in a NASA research center.

The space elevator

Imagine a ribbon stretching into space. The ribbon is 100,000 kilometers (62,000 miles) long and made of material that is 100 times stronger than steel. Imagine people and cargo being carried up this ribbon to an orbiting platform. This is a base from which you could set out to explore the **Solar System**. What you are imagining is the space elevator, and it may become a reality.

Platform in space

The main platform for the elevator will orbit Earth at a speed that matches Earth's rotation. This means that the elevator platform stays over the same point on Earth's surface. Communications **satellites** orbit in this way so that they always stay at the same point in the sky. This type of orbit is called **geosynchronous orbit**. Geosynchronous means "at the same time as Earth."

A cable would be lowered from the platform to an anchor point on Earth. This anchor would probably be a floating base in the ocean. From the space platform, the cable would extend thousands of miles even farther into space. There, it would be attached to a counterweight to balance the anchor and help keep the cable steady.

Laser-powered lifters

Lifting platforms will move up and down the cable, powered by electricity from laser beams. The lifting platforms would be able to take materials into orbit much more cheaply than sending them by rocket. In one day, the elevator could send up enough material to build a whole space station. With this cheap lifting power, people could build hotels and all kinds of other structures in space.

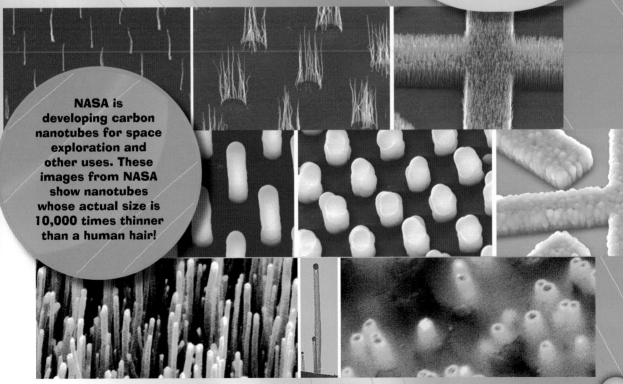

NASA is developing carbon nanotubes for space exploration and other uses. These images from NASA show nanotubes whose actual size is 10,000 times thinner than a human hair!

SPACE EXPLORATION TIMELINE

1543 Nicolaus Copernicus publishes a scientific **theory** showing that Earth and other planets **orbit** the Sun.

1609 Galileo Galilei uses an early telescope to view distant objects in space.

1687 Isaac Newton sets out his ideas about **gravity**.

1903 Konstantin Tsiolkovsky publishes a book showing that space travel is possible.

1926 Robert Goddard launches the first liquid-fuelled **rocket**.

1942 Germany launches the V2 rocket, the first human-made object to reach space.

1957 The USSR launches *Sputnik 1*, the first **satellite**.
The dog Laika becomes the first living creature to orbit Earth, aboard *Sputnik 2*.

1958 The United States launches its first satellite, *Explorer 1*.

1961 Yuri Gagarin becomes the first person to orbit Earth.

1962 John Glenn becomes the first U.S. astronaut to orbit Earth.
Mariner 2 is the first **space probe** from Earth to reach another planet (Venus).

1964 *Mariner 4* sends back the first close-up images of another planet (Mars).

1969 *Apollo 11* astronauts Neil Armstrong and Edwin Aldrin become the first people to land and walk on the Moon.

1977 *Voyager 1* is launched to explore deep space.

1980 *Voyager 1* reaches Saturn and sends back the first detailed pictures of the planet.

1981 The first space shuttle **mission** takes place.

1990 The Hubble space telescope is carried into orbit by the space shuttle.

2000 The first crew begin to live and work aboard the International Space Station.

2004 *Stardust* meets the **comet** *Wild 2* and collects sample of dust from its tail. *Spirit* and *Opportunity* begin their exploration of Mars.

2005 *Huygens* space probe lands on the surface of Titan, one of Saturn's moons.

2009 *Voyager 1* has traveled more than 16 billion kilometers (10 billion miles) from Earth. Kepler telescope is launched into space.

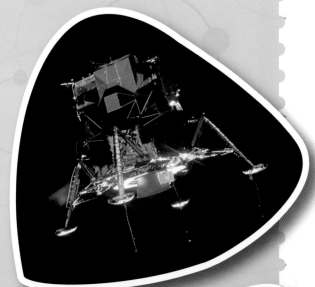

Space Quiz

1. Who launched the first modern **rocket**?
 a. Yuri Gagarin
 b. Konstantin Tsiolkovsky
 c. Robert Goddard
 d. Nicolaus Copernicus

2. What is a **supernova**?
 a. a shrunken star
 b. an exploding star
 c. a **satellite** of Venus
 d. a **galaxy**

3. Who was Edwin Hubble?
 a. the inventor of the telescope
 b. the **astronomer** who discovered the expanding universe
 c. the astronomer who discovered distant galaxies
 d. the scientist who discovered **gravity**

4. Which human-made satellite was the first to **orbit** Earth?
 a. *Sputnik 1*
 b. *Mariner 2*
 c. *Explorer 1*
 d. *Vostok 1*

5. How was the space shuttle different from other spacecraft?
 a. it carried a crew
 b. it came back to Earth
 c. it was reusable
 d. it was launched without rockets

6. On which planet are there rovers sending information back to Earth?
 a. Jupiter
 b. Saturn
 c. Mars
 d. Venus

7. Which invention advanced the course of space exploration?
 a. the telescope
 b. the **space probe**
 c. the rocket
 d. all of the above

8. How far is a **light-year**?
 a. 300,000 kilometers
 b. 9.5 million million kilometers
 c. 4.3 million kilometers
 d. 9.5 million kilometers

See page 47 for answers.

Glossary

accelerate cause to move faster

antimatter opposite or negative of matter. Antimatter consists of antiparticles, which are opposites of the particles that make up matter.

asteroid rocky object that orbits the Sun

astronomer person who studies astronomy. Astronomy is the scientific study of everything that lies beyond Earth's atmosphere, including planets and other objects in space.

atmosphere layer of gases that surrounds Earth and other planets

atom small piece of matter that everything is made up of

axis line around which a sphere rotates, such as the line on which Earth spins

black hole region of space formed by a collapsing star where the pull of gravity is so intense that not even light can escape it

capsule spacecraft made to carry people or objects safely in space

carbon nanotubes extremely tiny tubes made from the element carbon. These microscopic fibers are stronger than steel.

civilization group of people who developed a culture and society in a certain period

comet one of a number of objects in the Solar System that measures a few kilometers across and is made of ice and dust. When its orbit brings it close to the Sun, gases boil off the comet, producing a gassy tail.

constellation pattern of stars in the sky

data sets of information collected over a period of time

dense having parts that are very close together or concentrated in a small area

event horizon boundary of a black hole. Nothing can escape from inside the event horizon.

evidence visible signs that act as proof of an idea or belief

extravehicular activity (EVA) activity done by an astronaut outside the spacecraft. Also called a spacewalk.

galaxy huge system of billions of stars. The star we call our Sun is part of the Milky Way galaxy.

geosynchronous orbit orbit in which a satellite orbits Earth at a speed that matches Earth's rotation, so the satellite stays in the same place above the planet

gravity force of attraction between all objects in the universe

hypothesis unproved idea that is the basis for investigation

infinite going on forever without any limit or ending

laser beam very powerful beam of light

lens curved piece of material, such as glass or clear plastic, used to create an image

light-year distance that light travels in a year

Milky Way galaxy that contains our planet Earth and our Solar System

mission task or project

module unit of a spacecraft that is independent but fits together with other parts

nebula term used by astronomers to describe a cloudy patch of light in space. The first nebulae seen from Earth were galaxies. More powerful telescopes have since revealed nebulae that are vast areas of gas and dust in space.

neutron star star that has collapsed to become incredibly dense after a supernova explosion

orbit path followed by an object in space, such as a satellite or moon, as it travels around a larger object

parallax apparent shift of an object against a distant background when seen from different points of view

particle accelerator machine that breaks up atoms to make antimatter

polar regions areas around the geographic poles of a planet or moon

projectile anything that is set in motion by being thrown or fired, such as a rock or a rocket

propel push or drive something onward

propellant anything that is used to move an object, such as the fuel in a rocket or an aircraft

radiation energy given off by atoms as invisible waves or particles

radio wave type of electromagnetic wave, which is a wave of energy moving through space. Light and X-rays are other types of electromagnetic waves.

rocket something that is propelled through the air by the thrust created by burning gases; or the engine that produces the thrust

satellite object that travels in a circle around another object, such as the Moon traveling around Earth. It is also a human-made object sent into space to orbit Earth or another planet.

singularity beginning of the universe, according to the Big Bang theory. At this time, all matter, energy, time, and space were squeezed into a single incredibly small point.

solar panel device that converts the Sun's energy into electricity

Solar System the Sun and the family of planets and other objects in orbit around it

space probe unmanned spacecraft that is sent out to explore space beyond Earth and maybe beyond the Solar System

supernova star that explodes violently at the end of its life

theory idea that explains why or how something happens. If theories in science are tested and proved many times, they become accepted as facts.

thrust force that propels a rocket. The faster the jet of gas produced by a rocket engine, the greater the thrust.

Find Out More

Books

Aguila, David. *Planets, Stars, and Galaxies: A Visual Encyclopedia of Our Universe.* Des Moines, IA: National Geographic Children's Books, 2007.

Garlick, Mark. *Atlas of the Universe.* New York: Simon and Schuster Children's Publishing, 2008.

McGowen, Tom. *Space Race: The Mission, the Men, the Moon.* Berkeley Heights, NJ: Enslow Publishers, 2008.

Miller, Ron. *Rockets.* Minneapolis, MN: Lerner/Twenty-First Century Books, 2008.

Websites

http://amazing-space.stsci.edu/tonights_sky/
Amazing Space: Tonight's Sky
Watch a show about which constellations and stars to look for in the night sky this month.

http://www.newton.dep.anl.gov/askasci/astron98.htm
Ask a Scientist—Astronomy Index
Read hundreds of questions and answers from the Ask A Scientist Service at the Argonne National Laboratory. You can also ask your own question on this website.

http://hubblesite.org
HubbleSite home page
Learn more about Hubble and look at spectacular space images on the gallery pages.

http://mars.jpl.nasa.gov/funzone_flash.html
Mars Exploration—Fun Zone!
Find games, activities, and fun facts all to do with Mars.

http://www.jodrellbank.manchester.ac.uk/visitorcentre/
Jodrell Bank Centre for Astrophysics
Explore astronomy and the night sky.

http://www.nasa.gov/missions/calendar/index.html
NASA—Mission Calendar
Check this month's calendar for up-to-date mission information, and find links to past, present, and future NASA space missions.

Quiz Answers

1. **c** 2. **b** 3. **b** 4. **a** 5. **c** 6. **c** 7. **d** 8. **b**

Index